GOD'S ARCTIC ADVENTURER

GOD'S ARCTIC ADVENTURER

The Story of William Bompas

by

CONSTANCE SAVERY

LUTTERWORTH PRESS
GUILDFORD AND LONDON

ISBN 0 7188 1993 4

PRINTED IN GREAT BRITAIN
BY EBENEZER BAYLIS AND SON LTD.
THE TRINITY PRESS, WORCESTER, AND LONDON

CONTENTS

1

ROVING COMMISSION

A LONE traveller was crossing the Rocky Mountains. It was August, but a fierce freak snowstorm had blown up, whirling till the mountains looked as though they were fringed with white hair. For three days the traveller staggered blindly forward in the intervals between gusts of bitter furious wind that forced him to take refuge, again and again, in any rock cranny he could find. He had just spent two weeks in a gruellingly hot voyage up the Porcupine River from Fort Yukon. And now—this!

The traveller was William Carpenter Bompas on his way to England for the express purpose of telling the Church authorities that he did not want to be a bishop . . .

*   *   *

Eight years earlier, William Bompas had responded to an urgent public appeal for a volunteer to take charge of the Christian work at Fort Yukon on the Arctic Circle, where the missionary, the Reverend Robert McDonald, was believed to be dying.

Determined to get at least as far as Fort Simpson

before winter closed in, he had set out on the journey of eight thousand miles at the shortest possible notice and with the smallest possible amount of luggage. Battling for over five months against long delays, reluctant boatmen, dense forests and ice-blocked rivers, he had arrived triumphant at Fort Simpson on Christmas Day.

There were cries of amazement from everyone. Never before had a traveller ventured so far north so late in the year.

"But—" began the resident missionary-chaplain, the Reverend William Kirkby.

The other William waited expectantly.

"You haven't heard, then? McDonald has made an unexpected recovery. He is quite well now, and will not hear of relinquishing his work."

So he was not needed in Fort Yukon! Temporarily, the bottom dropped out of William's world. What was to become of him, he wondered.

For the moment, the answer was plain enough. He couldn't go forward and he couldn't go back. Till the winter was fairly over, he must stay where he was.

If he had been an unwanted guest, the situation would have been painful. But the Chief Officer and his men were delighted to welcome William, dropping in so unexpectedly with his news from the outer world to relieve the drearily monotonous and tame life at the Fort. He was like a breath of fresh air on that Christmas Day.

Like all the Hudson Bay Company's fur-trading posts, Fort Simpson had been built in days when it was feared that the Post might have to be defended against hostile Indians. When William saw that the half-finished church and the school-room for Indian and white children were on land outside the stockade, he knew that the Post was a fort in name only, visited by peaceable Indians who came to trade furs and to bring supplies of meat and fish for the Company's men.

Below the Fort's high embankment lay the frozen Mackenzie River, its surface littered—until the deep snow hid all from sight—with ice-boulders large and small, fantastically shaped into the likeness of monstrous beings, or severed human heads, or crested waves in the act of curling over. Around on every side pressed the dark woods where the Indians were encamped, some in deer-skin tents, others on open spaces cleared of snow, strewn with pine-branch "brush" and warmed by pine-log fires.

There were pine-log fires too in the sturdy little mission house where William worked hard at learning the Slavé and Cree languages whenever he was not helping William Kirkby by taking services in the Church or by visiting the Indian encampments during the short daylight hours that in winter lasted only from ten o'clock till two.

In those early days he was much distressed by what he called "the miserable way" in which the

Indians lived. Cold seemed to mean nothing to them: many families would not trouble to build themselves shelters when the temperature (Fahrenheit) had fallen from its usual ten or twelve degrees below zero to forty or even fifty. To make matters worse, they would persist in wearing, to William's disgust, "flimsy European dress" instead of their comfortable furs and skins. But he was glad to see that at least they had plenty of food to eat.

At times game and fish were so scarce that Indians and white men alike very nearly starved; but during William's first northern winter, supplies were abundant. True, it was not such fine fare as William had enjoyed at the Rapids when he was making his way north. His hosts, kindly French monks, gave him good bread made from fish roes, wonderful creams from the milk of the cow they had cleverly managed to keep alive, and plentiful preserves from the many kinds of delicious wild berries abounding in their neighbourhood.

No, the meals in Fort Simpson could not quite come up to that standard! However, each man could count on a good-sized fish for breakfast, moose or deer's meat with potatoes for dinner and rabbit as a rule for supper. If rabbit was served at mid-day dinner instead of supper, the allowance was a whole rabbit each.

William wintered quietly in his white world streaked with dark pines. The next few months were spent in teaching Indian orphans at Fort

Norman, three hundred miles further north. Then Kirkby and McDonald met to discuss his future. From what Mr. Kirkby had seen of him, it was decided that William Bompas was better suited for moving around the country than for staying a long time in one spot. He was to be granted what the two seniors termed "a roving commission".

So for the next eight years William roved. The Hudson Bay Company's trading-posts were from a hundred to three hundred miles apart, each having its bands of Indian hunters attached to it. Now William was to be heard of at Fort Rae . . . now at Fort Resolution . . . now at Fort Chipewyan . . . now back again at his headquarters, Fort Simpson . . . In spring, summer, and autumn months and far into the winter he went roving by dog-sledge or canoe.

*   *   *

Over the vast white spaces came the tinkling sound of bells as the dogs in their gay *tapis* (harness) sped across the snow. William was running beside the loaded sledge. If the way was open before him and no Indians were to be found, his snowshoes would easily cover from twenty to twenty-five miles before nightfall. It would be pleasanter to join the company round the camp fire or to pitch his own camp close by; in the absence of camp and company, he would sleep, as he had often slept before, in a deep hollow in the snow, with the side of the sledge to act as windbreak. When, on one occasion, his anxious sisters Selina and Sophia wrote from England to beg him not to risk his health by such a foolish practice, his next letter assured them that they need not fuss over him. A snow bed, if properly made, was safe and comfortable. "The warmest blanket is a snow blanket," William assured the worried pair.

This was no doubt true for a man like William, who was at all times ready to give anything he possessed to anyone who might appear to need it more. He met many such people in his eight years of roving.

For this night, at least, he would not need to test the warmth of his snow blanket. Away on the horizon his keen eyes could now pick out a cluster of tents with a thin blue column of smoke rising above them. The dogs sped on.

In the camp, everybody was quietly busy. Men were mending their fish-nets and repairing sledges. Boys were shaping bows and arrows. The old women slowly twisted grass or animal sinews into twine that could be used for making new nets or for sewing. Some of the younger women were dressing deer and beaver skins; others were fashioning ornamental belts and other articles from beads and porcupine quills.

They greeted William warmly; for it was not the first visit he had paid to this camp. Soon he was as busy as his friends. His dogs had to be cared for, and those that had lost their little moccasins during the run must have their toes examined for the lumps of hard snow and ice that would lame them if not gently removed. Yapping excitedly, the animals watched the unloading and preparing of their meal of porridge mixed with well-chopped dried fish.

The sick too had to be tended. For the invalids in the camp William had brought the "medicines" they loved best: chocolate, which they called "ox's blood" because of its dark colour; rice, their "white barley"; and the flour that they took to be "ashes from the end of heaven".

After the evening meal, William was free to say what he had come to say. He had not much time for speaking; a few hours more, and he would be on the trail again, searching for yet another group of hunters. It was unwise to stay long in any camp, for the Indians were constantly on the move in search of food or furs. Moreover, they could not be hurried; they needed slow, careful teaching if they were to take in the new thoughts that he was presenting to them. Small portions of Gospel truth were all that he could give during any one visit; but there was hope that the short Scripture lesson and the simple prayers and hymn-verses would have a better chance of being heard here in the white loneliness than in the hustle and bustle of a trading-post, where gains and bargains were all that mattered.

His friends listened and even asked questions that showed how well they remembered what he had taught them when they last met. By the flickering light of the camp fire William noted down some words and expressions that were new to him. Close by, his socks and shoes were drying in readiness for the next day's travel. An hour later, wrapped in blankets, he was asleep in a corner of one of the tents. With the dawn, he was loading his sledge again.

*   *   *

Another camp had been sighted, and William was being welcomed as warmly as before—but not, he feared, for the right reason. Though he was without medical training, he had somehow or other earned the reputation of being a first-class "medicine man"—and his arrival was immediately followed by the impromptu opening of a branch of a new kind of welfare and health service. The Indians flocked round him, clamouring for treatment.

Their attitude troubled William, as it had troubled him in the past and would often trouble him in the future. He reminded himself that he was a messenger charged with the most important message any man would ever hear: *God so loved the world, that He gave His only-begotten Son, that whosoever believeth in Him should not perish, but have everlasting life.* And sadly, William Bompas wondered, had he journeyed so many thousands of miles only to find that his Indian friends were so much interested in the healing of the body that they had little or no interest in the healing of the soul?

There was no way round the difficulty. A doctor they thought him, and a doctor he had to be, treating injuries and ailments and prescribing such needful remedies as calomel, jalap, quinine, laudanum, eye-drops, soap, grains of alum and raspberry leaf tea. At last all his patients were satisfied and the make-believe surgery could be shut for the rest of his stay. William sighed with relief. This time he had found no serious cases, no emergency with which he couldn't cope. And the invalids had been so co-operative and so grateful. It had been quite a different story when he had been called on, during a smallpox epidemic, to vaccinate five hundred Indians who strongly disapproved!

If William had been gifted with foresight, he would have shuddered at the task that lay ahead of him when he, an amateur surgeon if ever there was one, had to save a man's life by amputating his leg.

The injured man's friends stood waiting while William pondered the problem of how to do a major operation without an instrument of any kind. Presently William spoke—"Has anyone here got a handsaw?—Yes? Then give it to me please."

Using a common handsaw, he successfully amputated the leg. The man made a good recovery.

Fortunately for himself, William was not possessed of second sight, and so he missed this uncomfortable peep into the future.

*   *   *

"Ah! We come to the camp," proclaimed the Eskimo boy, dropping the hand of the blind man whom he had led for three days. "Here is a house where you can rest."

Glad to be out of the springtide's sun-glare, William Bompas stumbled into the darkness and lay down on the deerskins in the upper half of the one room. Snowblindness was agonizing while it lasted, and the accepted remedy—one drop of laudanum—felt like liquid fire when it was applied. But he knew that the blindness usually passed off within a week. Tomorrow he might perhaps be up and about again.

His roving commission had brought him to an unbelievable land where all the year round the earth was frozen solid a few inches below the surface, a land where no tree could grow and where berries seldom ripened on the bushes that were so rare as to be almost natural curiosities. Yet here, in this desolate region, the summer would bring butterflies—Sulphurs, Arctics, Alpines, Lesser Fritillaries, Coppers and Blues—the *ta-ka-lee-kee-ta* or "spots on the wings" of the Eskimos. It was amazing that their caterpillars could find enough Arctic plants to feed on.

Two days later, partially recovered, William was trying to get a little sleep when he was violently awakened by wild yells and dancing.

Indians in more fertile lands might if they pleased make medicines and ointments from blue-eyed grass, scarlet buffalo berries and bear's grease mixed with pitch from evergreens; but in the absence of most of these useful ingredients, the Eskimos had to obtain their results from spells and conjuring accompanied by ritual dancing.

Bursting out of his blankets and deerskins, William ran to put a stop to the intolerable din. He was said to be "as placid as the mountains and the lakes"—but evidently this was not one of his more placid moments. Anger bubbled over when he found an old Eskimo woman doctor busily engaged in curing a sick man.

"Your medicine-making is all a wicked lie!" he told the yelling dancer.

William paid heavily for his display of tactlessness and temper. The lady flew at him with her fists and nails . . . and . . . a bruised and battered William left that camp with more haste than grace. Later he had the satisfaction of meeting and of treating—in defiance of medical etiquette—the other practitioner's patient. The sick man was suffering from nothing worse than a sore head. Out of William's medical box came the grains of alum and the piece of soap with which he cleansed the

2

wound. They worked well. "Your conjuring is very strong," the smiling Eskimo told him.

*   *   *

Danger threatened William once more, but this time through no fault of his own, though a remote ancestor may have been partly to blame.

No one knows how the story of Cain and Abel had reached this the loneliest region on earth. But reach the Eskimos it did; for they had a tradition that way back at the beginning of the world two brothers had quarrelled, and one had murdered the other and was driven into exile. When white men first appeared on Eskimo ground, what was more natural to the Eskimos than to conclude that they must be descendants of the murderer?

With this thought curled up somewhere at the back of their minds, the Eskimos turned against William when everything went wrong at the beginning of their early summer voyage of two hundred and fifty miles, up the Mackenzie River to the Hudson Bay Company's nearest trading-post at Fort McPherson.

William had slept in their underground winter dwellings, had watched the building of their fairy beehive summer snow-houses, had fed contentedly on their whale blubber, rats, seal fat and raw slightly stale fish; he had hunted and fished with them; had helped to haul their sledges across the ice; he had taught them the Christian Faith as well

as a man could who did not know Eskimo as well
as he knew eight Indian languages. Yet their
suspicions of Cain's great-great-great . . . great-
grandson lingered still. When their voyage was
constantly hampered by blocks of floating ice,
dark looks were cast at William. One night he had
good reason to believe that they meant to murder
him.

It would be easy enough, and his body would
never be found. There were grim tales of headless
skeletons sitting for ages at the foot of trees in
Indian forests—but ice and snow could be trusted
not to reveal their secrets. William Bompas knew
he could do nothing to save himself. The words
My times are in Thy hand may have mingled with
his last waking thoughts of that night. After he
had said his prayers, he fell calmly asleep.

In the camp he had one staunch friend. Old
Shipataitook was not going to see the missionary
harmed. As William's enemies were making their
stealthy preparations, they heard a low voice
saying, "Wait! I have something to tell you. Last
night I had a very strange dream."

The would-be murderers knew better than to
pooh-pooh a dream. Who could tell what important messages might come in this way from the
grey shadowland of sleep? They waited.

"We had moved up the river," whispered Shipataitook, "and we were almost at Fort McPherson.
What do you think I saw? The banks were lined—

yes, lined—with the Hudson Bay Company's men and crowds of Indians, watching, watching. They were all armed, ready to shoot us down *if we did not have the white man with us!*"

It is not wise to inquire too closely whether Shipataitook truly dreamt a dream or whether he invented one for the occasion. Certainly this vision of his head upon his bed had an admirable effect. The murder-preparations stopped and everybody went peacefully to sleep. In the morning, bright smiles were seen in place of scowls. The puzzled William found himself being treated like a piece of eggshell china. All the way to Fort McPherson his companions were extra careful that no accident should happen to their missionary. How awkward it might be for all concerned if carelessness or clumsiness should cause him to tumble overboard!

In his letters home William made light of his perils and adventures. He was a great worrier about his work, and was for ever reproaching himself for slackness, spiritual "deadness", and for failure to hold the attention of his hearers; but dangers and fatigues meant very little to him. They could be dismissed in a sentence or two—"I have been nearly drowned and nearly frozen this winter already" or "I must have walked more than a thousand miles among the Indians this winter, but that is nothing . . ."

'Neath skies with stars that never set,
But round the pole still circle yet;
Where streamers of magnetic light
Enliven winter's lengthening night;
Where niggard suns must stint their ray,
To spend on climates far away;
There Christian brethren bend their knees
In shelter of the forest trees.
Hearts that with heavenly fervour glow
Are found amid the Arctic snow . . .

William was composing poetry, reciting it in a loud voice as he journeyed through wild and desolate places. Hard though he worked, he knew how to relax. In pre-Canadian days he had known nearly all Macaulay's *Lays of Ancient Rome* by heart. Now he made his own verses as he trudged along. Sometimes he would compose as many as two hundred lines in a day. These he would send home to be printed in missionary magazines, *The Gleaner* or *The Net*. And when, as sometimes happened, he was summoned to one or other of the Forts to take charge while a missionary went on leave, there would be a joyous holiday return to his books and above all to his favourite study: the Bible in Hebrew and Greek. A visit to a Fort might also bring him treasure in the shape of letter and parcels. Once, while staying in Fort Vermilion, he had the grandest of all his unpackings.

Before leaving England, William had hit on what

he regarded as a novel remedy for curing home-sickness. To keep his thoughts from straying back to his old life, he gave away or got rid of every personal possession—including his cherished paragraph Bible—that might make him think of home. Starting off with as little luggage as possible, he arrived at his journey's end only to find that letters and parcels would not be handed in at the door every day in the Far North, or that he might have to wait as long as three or even four years for a badly-needed book to reach him from England. There was to come a time when he felt grateful for the gift of a sweet-smelling lavender sprig enclosed in a home-letter . . . and there was another time when he would willingly have bartered everything he possessed—except his newly-bought Bible —for a bit of white chalk. It was of more use to him, he declared, than fifty gold sovereigns.

So, surrounded by boxes and bales, he dived into one box to discover those long-awaited books that he had ordered four years earlier for the use of the Hudson Bay Company's men: splendid illustrated Bibles, big bound volumes of popular magazines, *Good Words*, *The Leisure Hour*, *The Sunday at Home*, *The Quiver*. Another box held books and a dozen warm shirts from his kind old friend Mrs. Loft, Lady of the Manor in his first curacy. Sisters Selina and Sophia sent a much-prized Septuagint, the Psalms in Hebrew, and a Concordance. He was overwhelmed by the quantity of books, magazines, pamphlets, medical supplies, illuminated cards and pretty ornaments that were rained on him from other boxes. The finery of the dolls provided by Aunt Jane for his schoolgirls was "something amazing". A giver named simply "Mit" had sent needles, thread, scissors, bodkins, and soap. In his thank-you letters William was especially grateful for some adult reading-books given by a sensible person who had understood that grown men did not like to be taught to read from baby books with such sentences as "the dog went to get a rat".

Perhaps somewhere in his Aladdin's treasure-cave William found his bit of white chalk.

But in the midst of all this wealth William's sensitive conscience began to prick him, and he hoped that the arrival of so much reading would not make him idle and indisposed to move about that winter.

He need not have felt uneasy. Many hours of those wintry days were spent in translating hymns and portions of the Bible into the eight languages that he had at his command; and as soon as the weather permitted, he was away again on his unceasing journeys. Crossing overland from Fort Vermilion, he went down the Hay River to Great Slave Lake. On the way he passed some magnificent almost unknown waterfalls to which he gave the name they bear to this day, Alexandra, in honour of the Danish princess who had recently been wedded to Queen Victoria's eldest son. Before their beauty William stood spell-bound.

"One of the wonders of the world," he called the scene. "The amber colour of the falling water gives the appearance of golden tresses twined with pearls, while in the spray was a rainbow reaching from the foot of the fall to the rock far above its brink."

*   *   *

The eight years had drawn to an end. William went far west beyond the Rocky Mountains. In the summer of 1873 his travels had taken him to the mighty Yukon River, flowing now between high forest-clad hills and now between rough rocks, its banks ablaze with lupins, vetches, bluebells and even with delicate ferns nestling surprisingly in the crevices of the rocks. It was then that a letter arrived with startling news.

His own bishop, Robert Machray of Rupert's Land, had been attempting the impossible task of overseeing a diocese that stretched from Red River Settlement to the farthest trading-posts on the Mackenzie River, a distance as great as that from London to Mecca. Now this huge diocese was to be divided into four parts, one of which would be known as the Diocese of Athabasca. Bishop Machray and the Church Missionary Society had chosen wandering William as Athabasca's first bishop.

What! he thought; give up his roving commission? Never! He must make the authorities understand once and for all that he was not suited to be a bishop, had no proper qualifications for such a mighty task, and didn't like the prospect of going around organizing things. But clearly, arguing by letter was out of the question; it would take too long. By canoe, foot-slogging and dog-sledge he must make the three-thousand-mile journey down to Winnipeg where Bishop Machray lived. William headed about and made straight for that three days' ordeal in the Rocky Mountains . . .

2

TRAMP AT THE DOOR

"THERE'S a tramp at the door, asking to see you at once," the servant told Bishop Robert Machray. "Very persistent, he is."

It was New Year's Eve. Bishop Machray was hard at work in his study in Bishop's Court, Winnipeg. He did not want to be disturbed just then. "Take the man into the kitchen and give him something to eat. No doubt he's hungry."

The servant hesitated, but the Bishop put his head down and would not look up from his books. With another murmur of "very persistent", the man went out.

As he had foreseen, the tramp was not pleased at being taken into the kitchen: he kept on insisting that he must see the Bishop then and there. In the end he accepted the plateful of hot soup that was set before him, but between spoonfuls he continued to argue. He made so much noise that, the walls being thin, the Bishop was unable to go on with what he was trying to do. At last he laid down his pen and came out to the kitchen to remonstrate with the troublesome tramp. Pausing in the doorway, he took a hard look at his very lean, very tall, very voluble guest in the old fur cap, torn deerskin suit, leggings caked with swamp mud and aged moccasins. And then—

"Bompas!" he cried, hurrying forward, "is it you?"

Where clothes were concerned, William did not practise what he preached. He praised some Indian tribes for the thrifty way they kept their Sunday clothes in cedarwood boxes year after year so that they always looked as good as new. Other tribes he accused of wastefulness and extravagance. Some Indians, he observed severely, thought nothing of buying "a fine black suit", which got itself slashed to ribbons in their next journey through the woods. William himself was apt to be as tattered as his Indian brothers.

Back in the study, William and his host talked and prayed together. Out poured the troubled thoughts that had tormented William during the past eight years when he was struggling in loneliness to keep his soul alive in face of the "deadening influences" of indifference, ignorance and sheer wickedness by which he was constantly surrounded. There had been, he pleaded, so little "visible fruit" from his labours. "Before I entered on missionary work I had supposed it very favourable to heavenly mindedness and had pictured missionaries to myself as half angelic. I still hope others may find it so, but with regard to myself I regret to say that I have found my position not nearly so favourable to religious devotedness as ministerial work at home . . . I feel myself to be quite unworthy of so much attention and should be glad sometimes to suppose myself unnoticed and unobserved of any . . ."

Bishop Machray reasoned with him, but still William was not persuaded into accepting the call to be the chief shepherd of a diocese three thousand miles in length and breadth. Perhaps his extremely low opinion of his spiritual state and mental abilities hindered him from deciding whether the call was from God or only from man. When they parted, Bishop Machray's verdict on William was—"Bompas, a noble fellow, every inch of him a man, has just come in from the Arctic Circle, travelling four thousand miles in the last six months, and has gone on to England, where, *I hope*, he will be consecrated."

*   *   *

Wrapped in buffalo skins against the cold, William was an outside passenger in the coach that was taking him on a further stage of his journey to Portland, where he would embark for the voyage to England. No railway had as yet reached little Winnipeg, then a township of only three thousand souls, and travellers to Montreal and Portland had to resign themselves to changing from stage-coach to train twice over. Behind William, in the first of the stage-coaches, lay seven snowy days, followed by a dismal ice-cold journey in the first of the trains, ending in a snowdrift, out of which the engine had to be dug before two relief-engines could tow it to its destination. The experience had not been pleasant, and William sat on the top of his second coach saying to himself—

"Coaches and railway trains may be all very well, but dogs may be counted to hold their own in competing with horse-flesh or steam, whether on land or water. Give me a good dog-train any day!"

Snow lay deep as far as the eye could see. Now the horses were straining to scale a mountainous snowdrift. Could they make it? William and his fellow outside passengers held their breath. A moment later—whoosh!—and William and the others were flying through the air to land sprawled like star-fishes in a field. They sat up and rubbed the snow out of their eyes.

"Where's the coach gone?" one of the passengers asked dazedly.

"There, don't you see the wheels sticking up? Must have been a ditch somewhere under that snowdrift!"

Vigorous grumbles were heard. William had a mild rebuke ready. "Think! We have not been injured in any way; for the snow has provided us with a sufficiently soft bed to fall on. The inside passengers have had a more uncomfortable shaking. What cause have *we* to complain?"

As they tackled the job of releasing the bruised inside passengers and heaving the coach right way up, the outsiders thought they had plenty of cause. And even the intrepid William confessed to feeling "some apprehension" when, safely established in his second train, he perceived that it was jumping off the rails as it neared Montreal. He was glad to see that the guard was provided with a powerful winch for replacing the carriages on the track.

At Portland he had further proof that dogs could compete more successfully with steam either on land or water. The masts, yards and decks of the *Scandinavian* were thickly coated and hung with ice. With half the steam cut off and speed reduced to a minimum to keep her from blowing up, she crawled for thirteen days before limping into Liverpool in February 1874.

*   *   *

Speeding to London, William begged the leaders of the Church Missionary Society to find some other bishop. They would not listen to his excuses. "You have the necessary physical strength to endure severe hardships and loneliness; you have the gift of languages; you have a mission and a message. Why do you hesitate and draw back?" they asked.

Everybody seemed so sure that he was called

of God to be the new bishop! At last he yielded.

The Consecration could not take place till May. In the waiting months William felt as ill at ease as might a Polar bear that had been brought from Arctic wastes to a small bear-pit in a zoo on an August day. He knew now why the Indian children were restless cooped up within walls. Little green and pleasant England was as bad as a schoolroom with windows set so high you couldn't see out of them. How tame, quiet and orderly life seemed after the wild freedom of Canada! People stared at his tall spare figure swinging through the streets. And he had forgotten how to talk to his own countrymen. If only the English had been more like the Indians, who never talked unless they had something worthwhile to say!

Happily he had much to do, apart from quietly preparing himself for his new work. There were friends and relatives to be visited—and among them he found a certain "Nina"—Charlotte Selina Cox—to whom it was surprisingly easy to talk and whom he soon married. He would have to go down to Lincolnshire to preach again in his old curacy, he would need to take a course of hospital lectures on the treatment and cure of snow-blindness and in addition supervise the printing of the translations of the Bible that he had made in the last eight years. That alone took some time; for in addition to making a complete translation of St. Mark's Gospel he had rendered portions of Scripture, prayers and hymns into seven different dialects or languages.

Besides all this, he had a number of commissions to do for settlers in Canada who longed for goods that could best be obtained in the Home country. No fewer than six people wanted him to buy them gold watches; and he had been too good-natured to refuse to buy a pair of corsets for another petitioner. That commission gave him more trouble than all the rest!

*   *   *

The day of the Consecration had come. On May the third 1874 the Archbishop of Canterbury and three other bishops gathered in the parish church of St. Mary, Lambeth, to consecrate John McLean Bishop of Saskatchewan and William Carpenter Bompas Bishop of Athabasca.

In the dark grimy London Church the strains of the old hymn *Veni, Creator* rang out:

> Come, Holy Ghost, our souls inspire,
> And lighten with celestial fire.
> Thou the anointing Spirit art,
> Who dost Thy sevenfold gifts impart . . .

and so on to the laying on of hands and the solemn Charge when the Bible was delivered into William's hands and he was bidden to be to the flock of Christ "a shepherd, not a wolf; to feed them, devour them not. Hold up the weak, heal the sick, bind up the broken, bring again the outcast, seek the lost . . ."

William Carpenter Bompas had become the first Bishop of Athabasca.

3

TIGHT FIT FOR WILLIAM AND HIS WIFE

"THIS is disaster! Six extra mouths to feed!—
to say nothing of the boat's crew, who'll eat
more than the six put together! And one week's
supplies in hand!"

"Six!—when we expected only Bompas and that
new wife of his and were hoping against hope that
they would get stuck at the Rapids or somewhere
for the winter! Well, I trust Charlotte Selina or
Nina or whatever she's called knows what she let
herself in for when she married Bompas! He could
live on a cheese rind once a week, I believe, but
can she? *Six!*"

While William and his bride Nina were busy
with their unpacking, a secret council-meeting
went on at Fort Simpson. Only Mr. Kirkby was
missing from it, for he had gone to take charge of
the mission at York Factory. Chief Officer
Hardisty was looking desperately worried. He and
his men had greeted the newcomers with a flag
of welcome, smiles and friendly handshakes—and
nobody had guessed that beneath the grins and the
gaiety the hearts of Fort Simpson's people were
quaking.

"Hardisty," groaned somebody, "why didn't you somehow or other get word to Reeve and his family to stay where they were?"

"Well, I like that! D'you take me for a mind-reader or a prophet or something of the sort? How was I to know that the Bompases would stop at Fort Providence, take the Reeves off and bring them here so that Bompas could ordain Reeve and leave him at Fort Simpson as permanent chaplain while he himself goes careering off to the Arctic Circle or the moon or wherever?"

"Eight people in the mission house!—it will be a mighty tight squash! All the same as sardines!"

"Bompas is used to it, he's lived with the Eskimos. But tell me the answer to our own pretty problem. How on earth are we going to provide for all this lot?"

On and on went the debate about ways and means.

"Perhaps," said a hopeful voice, "perhaps Mrs. Bompas has brought plenty of supplies with her. Otherwise it'll be a case of Old Mother Hubbard all over again—

> "When she got there
> The cupboard was bare—"

The owner of the voice hoped in vain. William and Nina were as short of supplies as the Fort itself. To satisfy their hungry and rebellious crew they had been obliged to part with their flour.

Their bag of rice had got wet and was inedible. By mistake their chief grocery box had been left behind and could not reach Fort Simpson for another year. They had no coffee, no cocoa, no cornflour, no starch.

Soon bread was rationed in William's first "bishop's palace". He and Nina each had one small slice a day, and all the other members of the household had "a good-sized piece" twice a week.

In addition Nina had one dry biscuit a day. She was not allowed to share it with the almost starving sledge-dogs, who skulked round the Fort searching for food and stealing everything they could lay paws on.

It was well that Nina could not look ahead into the New Year, when her one small slice of bread would be granted to her only every other day, and when she would have hard work to keep back tears at the discovery that those rascally dogs had devoured a treasured half-pound of butter. She was not much comforted by hearing that once upon a time three fine Stilton cheeses had vanished when their owner left them unguarded for a minute or two. And she felt quite ashamed to remember that she had been dreaming—yes, actually dreaming!—about a dish of potatoes, steaming-hot and floury-white.

After a while, relief came. Indian hunters arrived, bringing supplies for present though not for future needs. Now that the situation had eased,

William thought it safe to go on one of his long cold-weather trips, leaving Mr. Reeve in charge of the church and of the school that he had opened.

William was a good and patient teacher, who never tired of teaching children to read by the syllabic method, but Nina's ears grew weary of hearing "ba, be, bi, bo, bu; cha, che, chi, cho, chu" over and over again. She much preferred making a fur cap and warm wrapper for her husband to wear on the journey to Fort Rae, three hundred miles off, on the shores of Great Slave Lake. And the dogs for his three sledges must have their *tapis* gaily ornamented with ribbon-streamers and jingling bells!

He was a splendid sight in his wraps, thick dark flannel leggings, moccasins over two pairs of duffle socks, thick coat, large mittens of deerskin and fur suspended from his neck. Folded into his baggage was the deerskin "robe" for covering him at night: two skins sewn together and lined with a blanket. Nothing was wanting that could add to his comfort. Nina had even contrived a crocheted woollen nightcap, an unheard of luxury.

Away he went, running beside his dogs at such a pace that he was soon out of sight. As Nina waved him off on that beautiful clear morning aglitter with sunshine, she had no suspicion how perilous that journey was to be, or how near the travellers came to dying of hunger and exhaustion. For his part, William forgot about his trials as soon as he had reached his Indians with the message of God's love.

He might have felt a little dubious if a satellite-picture had been able to give him news of the gay doings in Fort Simpson during his absence. Thanks to the Indian hunters with their relief supplies, the Simpsonites now had enough food, though they were short of "grease", the frozen deer or moose fat that was used for making candles and soap. But how long would those supplies hold out? Was every ounce of them going to be stretched as far as it would go?

Yalti Betzani (Bishop's wife) left the future to take care of itself. Under her direction, grand preparations were being made to entertain twelve old Indian women to a Christmas dinner of moose meat, rabbits, plum-pudding and tea. This effort was to be followed by a Christmas-tree with tea, biscuits and carols for the forty Indian and white children of the Fort.

In her childhood blue-eyed lively Nina had made so many toys for herself and other children that her mother laughingly prophesied that she would certainly be a toyshop keeper when she grew up. The prophecy looked like coming true that Christmas when she coaxed the men of the Fort to make drums, tops, whips with carved handles, balls and work-cases while she herself was engaged in dressing dolls of all kinds from a jolly Jack Tar to a baby in a proper Indian moss-bag cradle. Her clever fingers also fashioned dancing men moved by strings as well as a horned woolly lamb—Mackenzie River breed—with sparkling black eyes. Aprons and leggings delighted the older Indian girls, and beautiful gifts were found for their elders in the boxes she had brought from England.

Chief Officer Hardisty spared enough of his hoarded "grease" to make tiny candles, and the blacksmith made the little tin moulds for them. Not to be outdone, the schoolmaster contrived candlestands and bright flags and set up a large text *Peace on earth and goodwill towards men*. When all was ready, the tree glowed in the middle of a room decorated with fir, their only evergreen. There had never been such a Christmas at Fort Simpson before.

*   *   *

On a Sunday morning at the end of January William's sledge bells were heard again jingling across the snow. In he came, carrying with him the home letters for which Nina had been longing for eight whole months. Across the breakfast-table two unexpected little faces were smiling at him. The mission house's walls must surely have been made of elastic; for in William's absence Nina had taken charge of the motherless children of Brown the carpenter, who was obliged to be away from the Fort for a time.

William and Nina were never to know the joy
of having children of their own. The small Browns
were the first children to come under their care.
But the Browns were not the last. No, not by
dozens!

4

MORE LONG TRIPS

As they were preparing for next day's hunting-trip, the small band of Indian hunters looked up to see the Bishop bearing down on them.

"I hear that a camp has lately been pitched about twenty miles off, in the direction you're going. Could you let me put my camping-gear on one of your sledges? Mine's out of action; for I can't get hold of any of the dogs from the Fort. As you know, they are all being used for hauling wood just now.'

The hunters nodded assent. "You're welcome, Bishop. We're starting early to-morrow, soon after five."

When Nina heard of the proposed trip, she felt anxious, though there seemed no reason for anxiety. The trip was not a long trip covering thousands of miles or even a medium-sized trip of a few hundreds, but one of the shortest he had taken. Lone travelling could be dangerous, but this time he would have plenty of company. Yet still the anxiety persisted. In the end she sent a private message to a young hunter whom she knew, a steady boy who supported his widowed mother and sang in the choir. "Please take care of the Bishop," Nina begged.

Natsatt sent a return message. He sounded slightly offended. "Tell Yalti Betzani, is *he* not our Bishop, and are *we* not men? *Koka!*" (That's enough!)

So at five o'clock on a cold, blowing, snowy February morning William sat down to enjoy a breakfast cooked by Nina. The temperature had risen, he was glad to note. During the night it had been fifty degrees below zero, but it was now only thirty degrees below.

In semi-darkness the sledges drew up at the mission house. William's blankets and cooking-pot were loaded on to one of them, and he ran alongside as he had done so often before. For ten or twelve miles he kept up with the hunters. The temperature dropped ten degrees. Then, exhausted by the bitter cold and biting wind, he lagged behind and was soon out of sight.

"Something's wrong!" shouted Natsatt. "I don't feel easy. I'm going back."

Turning, he skimmed lightly over the snow. Soon he spied a white doubled-up heap in the middle of the track. William, in agony from snow-shoe cramp, was already half frozen. Death was a bare fifteen minutes away.

Natsatt acted swiftly. He rubbed the stiffened limbs, tore down pine branches, kindled a fire with flint, steel and country touchwood, and quickly gave William hot water to drink, Gradually the cramp loosened its grip and William could walk again, though very slowly.

Late that afternoon two men were seen approaching the Fort. One appeared to be an old man. Nobody recognized him as he dragged himself along. At the mission house Nina was shocked to see that the aged one was her husband.

*   *   *

Summer had come quickly to Fort Simpson. On May the thirteenth the rivers were still icebound and the earth covered with snow. Within three weeks the gooseberry bushes were in blossom, and beneath larches of a delicious tender green the people of the Fort walked on carpets of wild strawberry blossom. There was hardly any night; for the sun did not set till ten p.m., and the four hours of twilight ended with the two o'clock dawn. But William and Nina had not much time for observing the beauties of nature. After he had recovered from the illness that followed his last adventure, he had made a prolonged tour round his enormous diocese, making plans as he went for new and old mission stations and schools. In the course of his many journeys he had found that after all Fort Simpson was not the best place for his headquarters; it was not central enough. Fort Chipewyan on Lake Athabasca was better. So he and his wife were hard at work packing their possessions, some of which would have to be left at Fort Simpson for the next twelve months.

The question was, which things were to be taken and which left. Whatever was most urgently needed in Fort Chipewyan was almost certain to be the one priceless treasure that was now stuck at Fort Simpson. It was a voyage of five hundred miles in the Hudson Bay Company's fur-transporting canoes, and Nina would make it alone save for the three Indian children who were now under her care, the youngest being a delicate motherless baby. William would be leaving on a northern trip to Peel River and the Yukon ten days before she went south.

Off glided the "brigade"—twelve boats—in stately style, loaded with bearskins, red and black fox, sable, lynx, mink and beaver. A month later Nina and her charges were established in another bishop's palace.

It had one large room, out of which a ladder led up to a small attic. Cooking had to be done in the yard, on a stove inside a skin tent. Here Nina lived, cared for her Indian children, taught school in a wooden shanty near the palace, and waited for William to come back from the missionary journeys that were to last many months.

When he came at last, Baby Jeannie was dying of tuberculosis and Nina was very ill. She had suffered so much from cold, hunger, hardship and loneliness that it was plain she must go, after

Jeannie's death, down to Winnipeg, a thousand miles away, where kind friends would nurse her back to health and happiness.

This was the first of several long absences from home through illness. Owing to the difficulties of travelling, the absences sometimes lasted for a year, once for five years. But always, as soon as she could contrive it, Nina Bompas came hurrying back to the palace again.

* * *

Letter in hand, William Bompas bent over a map tracing a route with his finger.

The letter was from the Bishop of Columbia Diocese, asking him to act as peacemaker at the other end of nowhere—an uncommonly awkward request.

Far away in Metlakahtla on the Pacific Coast a devoted but very headstrong missionary was giving the Indians some teaching that the Bishop of Columbia believed to be mistaken. He would not listen to what the Bishop said, but went his own way. Bishop Hill knew it was useless for him to go to Metlakahtla himself to plead with the missionary, who had unfortunately taken a strong dislike to him. Would William, a brother bishop, go instead?

As Nina was then being nursed back to health by the friends in Winnipeg, William knew that he was free to answer the call. He studied the map again. "I shall need a stout canoe and Indians to man it. We'll start from Dunvegan on the Peace River. It should take us about five days to reach Fort St. John. That is, if we aren't too badly hindered by drift-ice from the tributary streams. Then on to Rocky Mountain House . . . the Peace River Canyon's too risky to attempt, we'll have to avoid it by making a land portage of about twelve miles. There'll be some hard work after that, poling the canoe all the way to Parle Pas Rapids. Very swift current there, must look out for that. . . . McLeod's Lake Fort, we'll have to rest there for a bit before trying to cross the Lake. No good to overdo things! Another portage from Lake McLeod to Stuart Lake—whew!—it's every step of eighty miles! Fort St. James on the shores of the Lake, that will be a good place to stop at. Shouldn't wonder if I had trouble with the Indians at that point, they may not want to go any further if the weather's rough . . . Fort Babines next, and then a land trail over the mountains to Skeena Forks. I don't look forward to going down the Skeena. Glorious scenery on the 'river of mists'—but oh, what a river! And then—"

William's moving finger had reached Port Essington on the Pacific Coast.

"If I can reach Port Essington alive, the rest's easy enough—just a canoe-voyage of twenty-five miles along the coast. Nothing in it! Those Pacific breezes are mild enough at all seasons of the year, I'm told, and I hope it's true. But till I get to Port Essington it will be a race with winter!" said William to himself.

William always enjoyed a challenge. As long ago he had fought hard to reach Fort Simpson by Christmas Day, so now he was determined to win the race to Port Essington. He pushed the map aside and sat down to write the letter that would tell Bishop Hills that a rescue operation was about to begin.

*   *   *

Before William began his journey on a frosty October day, he spelt the word "winter" with a small letter. When he ended it nearly seven weeks later, he was spelling Winter with a capital; for in the meantime Winter had become a personage, a giant foe whose early frosts and snows had given him the first start in the race, and who followed the canoe relentlessly, pressing nearer and nearer with his dreaded drift-ice till at Fort St. John he unexpectedly fell behind and was seen no more for a fortnight. But Winter recovered his lost ground at Parle Pas Rapids, where the current was so strong that the canoe turned on its crew and was swept violently downstream. He filled the gorge of the Rocky Mountains with fog, and he filled McLeod's Lake with half-solid ice. It was Winter who froze the eighty-mile portage between Lake McLeod and Stuart Lake, and compelled the voyagers to stay at Fort St. James for four days while the ice was thickening on Stuart Lake and snowstorms were raging overhead.

William had anticipated trouble with the Indians at this point. Winter ensured that he got it. When William at last persuaded the Indians to attempt the crossing of the Lake, Winter revenged himself by sending down a terrific snowstorm. They reached Fort Babines only to be harassed again by deep snow on the land trail over the mountains. Winter was putting forth all his strength now, but he was mistaken if he thought William could be defeated by being forced to sleep in a foot and a half of snow and to cross the rugged mountain trail without snowshoes. Temporarily defeated, Winter had to stay behind when the travellers went down the sheltered western slope of the portage. Looking back, William thought he could see Winter frowning down on him from the heights.

When the Skeena was reached, it was easy to understand why Winter had frowned. Although by rights the "river of mists" should have frozen a fortnight earlier, in mid-November it was still open. Thankfully, William embarked, but he feared that Winter might still have weapons in store in the shape of great ice-boulders sent rolling after the canoe in cold pursuit. As it turned out, Winter took another weapon from his armoury, another violent and prolonged snowstorm. It failed, and the race was won. Scowling, Winter retreated to his mountain glooms.

A missionary named Morrison met William in Port Essington. William was looking—as his wife often remarked—"tattered and unpresentable". Morrison did not mistake him for a tramp, but he did take him for a gold-miner.

"Well," said Morrison kindly, "what success have you had?"

"I've been fairly successful," answered William.

Mr. Morrison suddenly saw that William was wearing the remains of what might once have been a bishop's attire. He remembered having heard a rumour that a bishop might be arriving shortly.

"Perhaps," he said doubtfully, "you are the bishop who was expected?"

"I'm all that is left of him," said ragamuffin William.

*   *   *

His sea trip of twenty-five miles brought the peacemaker to Metlakahtla. He did not find his task too hard. Gentle persuasion soon induced the rebel missionary to stop defying his bishop and to obey that bishop's reasonable requests. For the next four months William and the missionary worked happily together; and when William left the mission station it was with good hopes that everything would go well in future. And for some time afterwards, though not for ever, there was peace.

A steamer took William across to Queen Charlotte's Island to see his friend Collison, who was

4

stationed there. When the short visit was over, Collison and another missionary accompanied the Bishop for a little way along his homeward trail, as he was returning to his own diocese by a different route, through the woods to the head of navigation on the Naas River. Before they parted, they stopped under the great solemn trees to pray for a blessing on their threefold work for God.

Indians did not ask directly for any article they coveted: it was manners to point the finger at the desired object. Shabby though he was, William had still some possessions that an Indian would value. He gave away his great-coat and a cooking-pot before he plunged into the forest.

*   *   *

Terrible news met William on his return. Famine had struck again, harder than ever. The worst of the trouble was over now, but everywhere William could see signs of the past horror. Where there were no horses that could be killed for food, the Indians had been forced to eat the beaver-skins on which their future livelihood depended. Their haggard looks haunted William. Nor were the white men any better off. When he went to see his friends the McAulays, he was shocked to see their pallid baby daughter, who had very nearly died after eating a bit of bearskin. "We did our best," the anxious parents assured William. "It was carefully singed, boiled and toasted."

Worse than all, throughout those long months there had hovered over men's thoughts a shadow and a fear that desperate need would drive some poor human beings to feed on man's flesh. They would become outcasts, shuddered at and abhorred by their fellow Indians, who believed that cannibals turned into *weentigos*, witch-creatures with hearts of stone.

William acted quickly. The danger of starvation might be over for the present, but means must be taken to prevent hunger from striking again. His last long trip had shown him ways in which this could be done. The Pacific Coast missionaries were encouraging their people to grow potatoes, and had recommended him to do the same. He knew that potatoes would never ripen in the Far North; but when he came through the Peace River district he had seen splendid fertile land quite uncultivated. Why should not every mission station have its own farm on those rich grounds, run by a skilled farmer? This would give employment to the Indians; and perhaps they themselves would begin to cultivate their own farms when they found that cattle could be raised and barley, potatoes, vegetables and even wheat could be grown. True, there was a silly saying that no Indian would take up farming as long as he had a drop of red blood in his veins—but William paid no heed to that kind of nonsense!

Again, he had seen how useful steamers were on

the Pacific Coast. Why should not a mission steam-launch of about twenty horse-power be placed on the Mackenzie River, thirteen hundred miles of which were navigable. Supplies could then be brought when and where they were needed; trading goods could be carried up and down; and travel would be much easier.

Eagerly William set to work on his farming project in country that was later to become a great granary for two continents. Under his constant watchfulness the mission farms did well. If they are remembered now, it is because they played their part in the story of two of Canada's famous men, William Bompas and another.

When the Bishop was starting his farms, he chose as one of his helpers a notable young man of twenty, Sheridan Lawrence, who was afterwards to become a figure of such national importance that at his death the Government of Canada erected a memorial cairn in his honour. A bronze tablet on the cairn hails him by the title given to him in fun during his lifetime, *Emperor of the Peace*, and it goes on to state that he was "farmer, miller, meat packer, merchant, friend of the Indian, road builder, freighter, magistrate, patron of education; he embodied the endurance, enterprise, versatility and vision of the pioneer".

William's second venture—that of the steam-launch—was successful too—but in a decidedly roundabout way. The Hudson Bay Company put its foot down when the word was buzzed that the Bishop had plans for that busy little steam-launch on the Mackenzie.

"This will never do," said the directors of the Company. "We are the lords of the north. Our prestige among the Indians will suffer if the missionaries have a steam-launch when we have none."

William was made to understand that he better say no more about his steam-launch unless he wanted to offend the powerful H.B.C. He waited quietly: it may be that he suspected he would see ripples spreading out from the stone he had thrown into the pond. Sure enough, the Company presently built their own fleet of steamers, bigger and better than anything a poor missionary bishop could afford. Little did William care who got the credit for his bright idea. The steamers were puffing along the Mackenzie River. That was enough for him.

5

RESCUE OPERATIONS

AFTER she came back from Winnipeg, Nina Bompas gathered children round her once more. While her own health was failing she had lost frail Baby Jeannie, whom all her loving care could not save. But there were always others! The Bishop seldom returned from his long trips without bringing two or three Indian children whose parents wanted them to attend the schools he was setting up. They were not afraid to go away from home in the company of this stranger. He might be tall, spare, grizzled, with piercing eyes and a hawk nose—but they knew he was their friend and champion.

They could not have been more right. William could always be trusted to go to the rescue of any child in distress. Once, passing a schoolhouse, he heard the cries of a child who was being whipped. The Bishop thundered at the door for admittance. When his insistent knocking was not instantly answered, he burst the door open with a mighty shove, rushed into the room, snatched the culprit from its teacher, took it in his arms, and sat down to soothe and comfort it. What the teacher thought or said, nobody knows.

Then there was ten-year-old Jeannie de Nord, whose widowed father sent her to stay with an uncle and aunt while he went on a hunting trip. Bright-eyed, mischievous Jeannie was unhappy. One Friday she pretended to be going to fetch wood. As soon as she was out of sight, she ran in search of her father.

It was winter and starving wolves were on the prowl; but the uncle and aunt did not bestir themselves to go and look for Jeannie when she was late in returning from her chore. At night, it was plain that she had made off somewhere without food or blanket. "She'll come back when she's hungry," was all the aunt had to say.

Neighbours did not behave so airily. On the Saturday an Indian family told Nina that Jeannie was missing. Hurrying home, Nina told William, who organized a search-party and went off without waiting to put on extra clothing. No more was heard of him till between three and four o'clock on the Sunday morning when a knock brought Nina to the door.

There stood William, writhing in the agonies of snow-shoe cramp after wading through snow streams and walking for many miles in wet clothes. When at last he could speak, Nina asked him, "Did you find her?"

"Yes," William replied. "She had gone to an old deserted tent of her father's, looked about till she found a gun he had hidden, managed to get a

spark from it and so made a fire. She collected
brushwood for a bed and went to sleep. She wan-
dered about all day Saturday looking for her
father, and if she hadn't come back to the tent to
sleep, we might never have found her. As it was,
we nearly missed her; for she made no sign when
we fired to attract her attention. We fired towards
the mountains, so it seems the sound came upon
the child's ear from the opposite direction, the
one towards which she was seeking her father. She
thought that he would be sure to come to the tent
—so she never moved but went peacefully to sleep
again. She seemed pleased to see us when we
looked in and woke her up. '*Ti tin die!*' ('I'm
hungry'), she said, as soon as she saw us."

"Could she walk home?" Nina wanted to
know.

"What!—twelve miles? No, of course not. I
carried her nearly all the way. Oh yes, we had
remembered to give her something to eat! She's
all right."

If Jeannie was all right, William was not. The
rescue-operation meant several days of suffering
for him. But he would willingly have endured it
again if only he had been able to save her from
a sad end four years later. The wild little thing
had become a valuable assistant to the old hunter,
who made her work much too hard. One day,
when William and Nina had left that neighbourhood, he sent her to the woods with dogs and

sledge to bring back a deer he had killed. On her
return, the exhausted child lay down on her bed
to die.

* * *

Strictly speaking, it was not William who rescued
Owindia, the dearest of all their "children". She
came into the lives of William and Nina in a
strange way.

Baby Owindia lay crying on the river-bank. She
had lain there for seventeen hours, ever since her
father had murdered her mother. Nobody cared
what became of Owindia, whose name, "The
Weeping One", fitted her very well on that day.
She was nobody's business, just a lonely bundle of
misery.

A boat-load of Indians paddled past the scene of
the murder. Owindia cried on, hopelessly. One
man was touched by the sound of the little wailing
voice. He got out, picked Owindia up and took her
where he knew she would find a home. "She
spoke to my heart," he said simply as he handed
her in at the door of the Bishop's house.

Baptized Lucy May, Owindia lived long enough
to grow into a happy child, the darling of her new
parents throughout her short life. She was two
years old when William, contrary to his usual
custom, decided to take his wife with him on one
of his long trips. He had planned to go to distant
Fort Norman, which place he meant to use as a

jumping-off ground for visits to the northern tribes.

*　　　*　　　*

"Look, children, look! The Rocky Mountains!" said William.

There were two children in the small craft that was nearing Fort Norman. Caroline, aged ten, was the sister of the Indian teacher at the Fort, a grave, sedate little person. Owindia-Lucy-May was joyously alive. "She is as full of fun and mischief as a child can be," declared the proud mother.

Nina Bompas's own first view of the Rocky Mountains was marred by the sight of a great barrier of ice in the river, the first they had seen since they started on the trip early in June. She kept one apprehensive eye on the bold, rugged peaks, on whose snowy surface the morning sun gleamed and shimmered with exquisite effects, and the other eye on the large blocks of ice that were sliding down the river-banks with loud sounds as of thunder.

"We can't get to the landing-stage," said William, "and it looks as though we had better not stop here!"

The boat was hurriedly put back until a small, sheltered and fairly safe creek could be found, into which it was run and then moored to the top of the bank with a strong rope. For a day and a night they had to stay where they were, waiting for the ice to move. Above them, friendly Indians were cutting a track through the ice-blocks to the Fort, along which they would presently carry boxes and bedding.

But after many hours of listening to ice-thunder, William could stand the inaction no longer. "Nina, you and the children must stay here for the present; but if I wait any longer I shall not be able to talk to the Fort Indians before leaving on my first northerly trip. I simply can't afford to waste another day. There's a way through the forest that I can try if only I can get up this bank."

Once more he slithered and slipped and scrambled up the dangerous bank, and vanished into a tangled, thorny, trackless wood. Nina knew only too well what would happen before he reached the Fort. She sat in the boat with melancholy vision of the endless darning and patching she would have to do.

In the end, they all arrived at the mission house, which was nearly derelict and, as Nina remarked when she saw it, "so small that three sparrows might dance on the floor". It was also so cold that when winter brought William home from his trips he had to pad the interior with moss and paper, break old cases for turning into shutters, and to fix old sails overhead to keep out draughts. In summer, Fort Norman had all the advantages. The endless play of light and shade on the mountains was a delight. Fossils, crystals and gold could be found on the river banks; wild flowers and blueberries abounded. But in winter it was a place of dread.

*   *   *

Four men were tramping through the woods on their way to Fort Norman. From time to time they stopped to listen and to call the name of a fifth, who had gone after a bear earlier in the day and had not returned. At last the calling and the listening stopped. Much shaking of heads followed. "It's no use, he won't come now. I expect he has gone back to Little Rapid."

They walked on. After a time three of the party talked together, looking uneasily about them.

"What is it?" the fourth man asked.

"We're on the wrong track," came the reluctant answer.

The fourth man sighed. His companions had joined him at Little Rapid, only six days' journey from Fort Norman, but he had travelled two thousand, five hundred miles during the summer months and had spent the autumn visiting posts on the Liard River. Then from Fort Simpson to Little Rapid he had fought for his life on a clumsy little raft that was very ill-fitted for dodging, day after day, the Mackenzie River's thickening ice. He had won the battle, but victory had left him rather tired.

In the winter the moon shone gloriously for

sixteen hours. That night it lit up the rueful faces
of four men whose supply of provisions had been
intended to last for six days only. As they camped,
they silently calculated how much longer the
journey would last.

It took twelve days instead of six. On the
eleventh day they had no food left after a fish and a
small barley cake had been divided between four.
A few hours went by. Suddenly the fourth man
staggered and fell.

On rocky soil, late-ripening cranberries might
still be hiding under the snow, sweeter and
juicier than next summer's crop; but there were no
cranberries here in the forest. Nor was there any
sign of that other gift from heaven, the *tripe de
roche*, the black lichen that made a nourishing and
fairly palatable soup when boiled down into a
gelatinous mass.

The fourth man's companions did the best they
could for him. They kindled a fire, and hurried off
to fetch help.

*   *   *

Knock, knock, knock at the door of the mission
house in the middle of the night!

"What is it? Who is there?" cried startled Nina.

"We bring you tidings of Bishop. He is
starving!"

Nina's heart sank, but faith kept her steady. So
many times William's life had been at risk—and

all those many times God's loving care had brought him through. That care would not fail her now.

She was up and dressed in a flash. Then came the business of persuading the young Indian, Whu-tale to go in search of William, taking the needed food.

"Whu-tale, Bishop is starving in the woods. I send him meat—*chiddi, chiddi* (quick, quick). You take it to him, eh?"

Oh, if only Natsatt had stood there instead of Whu-tale! But Natsatt the brave and loyal was dead, drowned while hunting beaver. And all too plainly Whu-tale did not think the middle of the night was the best time for a rescue operation, especially as the thermometer stood at nearly thirty degrees below zero and starving wolves had been seen near the Fort. He looked at the floor. "Maybe to-morrow," he said helpfully.

Nina knew that death would not be kept waiting. "No, Whu-tale, to-morrow Bishop must be here. He cannot stand till he has eaten meat. I want you to take it now, and go to him like the wind. If you go directly and bring Bishop safe, I will give you a fine flannel shirt."

This bargain satisfied Whu-tale. "Then it would not be hard for me to go—and perhaps like the wind."

The larder of the mission house was empty of anything likely to put life into a starving man.

Without a thought for her own safety, Nina flung on her deerskin coat and went hurrying up the hill to pound on the door of the Chief Officer of the Fort. He woke from sleep to find the midnight caller urgently begging for moose meat. Then she was away down the hill again to hustle Whu-tale, his gun and his packet of food off the premises. With Whu-tale safely away, Nina sat down to wait. While she waited, she prayed . . . and after dark on the following day Whu-tale triumphantly claimed his flannel shirt. He had brought back the Bishop, fringed all over with icicles and more dead than alive, but quite undaunted. When travelling was next within sight of being possible, he was off again among the drift-ice.

"The breaking-up of the ice in spring in the large rivers is sometimes a fine sight," was his cool comment. "The ice may pile in masses along the banks to the height of forty feet . . . When any check occurs to the drifting of the broken ice, the water may suddenly rise to the height of fifty feet or more, and flood the country."

Fortunately for William, on his next expedition no such check occurred. A time was to come, not many years ahead, when he would not think the sight quite so fine.

6

THE Yukon Indian pointed with his finger to the dying camp fire in the forest clearing. Its glow had gone; it was nothing but a pale heap of ashes. Round it the long branches of the sentinel trees pointed their accusing fingers, too.

"That is how you have left us," he said to William. "Ten years ago you kindled the fire of the Gospel among us, and left it untended to die out again. Why have you done this?"

William stared at the dead fire. He felt hopeless. How could he explain that he had done all the travelling one man could do in regions where snow, ice and blizzards made it impossible for many months of the year? The Yukon in particular was said to be composed of "three months of mosquitoes and nine months of snow". The Indians might just as well have blamed him for failing to catch one particular fish out of all the fishes in the Pacific Ocean! At that very moment, was he not doing one of his tremendous trips along the northern waterways? And he knew that in every one of those trips he had done his best to kindle and tend the Gospel fire.

But the Yukon Indian's words did serve to impress on him—though he needed no impressing! —that one man's best was not nearly enough. During the next few days, he spent his few spare moments sitting on a log, writing letters on blue sermon-paper, in the handwriting that had something of the graceful easy-flowing curves of the Mackenzie River. They were urgent letters such as he had often written before, but now their note of urgency was more marked than ever. Men were needed in these northern wilds, many men. Money must be provided for their support. And the Diocese of Athabasca was far, far too large to be left to one chief pastor. At all costs, it must be divided.

His appeals were heard and answered. Men and gifts of money came from England. One very generous gift provided the Eskimos with their own special missionary. Some time later William discovered that this gift came from his own brother, George.

After much pressing, he got his way about the division of the diocese. Athabasca was split in two. The smaller, southern part kept the old name of Athabasca. The larger, northerly part became the Mackenzie River Diocese. It stretched to the Arctic Circle, remote and wild.

William was allowed to have his choice. No one who knew him would be surprised that he chose the hard way—Mackenzie River.

As before, he journeyed in spring, summer and autumn. His winters were spent here, there and everywhere, if not in his own mission house, then in an empty log cabin, or in a schoolroom, or in the corner of a log church. Wherever travelling was humanly possible, there William went.

*   *   *

Among the mountains the wind roared and rattled and raved. There was no other sound in the whole white wintry landscape. From the windows of a little church the yellow gleam of candlelight shone over the wide waste of snow.

Inside the church, William Bompas sat on a box of books by the stove, writing in a manuscript book that was slipped between well-worn oilskin covers. His few possessions were ranged in neat order near him: iron cup, tin plate, knife, kettle, blankets —and very little else. Wintering fifteen hundred miles from the frontier border of Canadian civilization, he looked on a piece of dried-yeast bread as his sweetest luxury. He gave away anything that was needed by anybody else, be it food, hat, or blanket. It was said that he once gave his trousers to an impoverished Indian and marched home in his red flannel underwear.

He was busy as usual with the sermon preparation, letter-writing and reports that occupied the dark hours.

When his work was done, he laid aside his pen

and picked up his New Testament. This was the best part of the day: he was about to sit down to what was better to him than a feast.

His love for the Bible grew deeper every day. He enjoyed reading it in English and in Greek; and when he first read the Old Testament in Hebrew he remarked, "It seemed almost as though I saw an angel's hand tracing for me Hebrew sentences, as on the wall of Belshazzar's house".

But on that cold, cold night William was not reading the Bible in English, Greek or Hebrew. He was exploring what he called "a new world of wonders".

For a long time he had wanted to study the New Testament in Syriac, a very ancient version used by Syrian Christians. He believed that the Syrian language, so like the Aramaic spoken by our Lord Himself, would reveal His words in their full beauty, making of them "a pure fountain of joy".

And to his supreme delight Nina, far away in England, had sent him a Syriac New Testament and lexicon. Night after night he studied his treasure, noting down the discoveries he made, and preparing for the time when he would make a new translation from Syriac back into English. In the thank-you letter written to Nina, he told her, "The Syriac text leads me nearer to God than all the commentaries I have ever read."

Both before and after he got his Syriac New

Testament William did a great deal of book making. His early translations were followed by others in the Slavé, Beaver, Dog-Rib, Chipewyan and Tukudh languages. For his Indians he had also translated parts of the Prayer Book and had prepared reading-books and books of hymns and prayers. When money was wanted for building churches and schools, he helped to raise it by writing an account of the Mackenzie River Diocese that is still in use today as an important source-book of Canadian history. His verses still travelled to England to be printed in missionary magazines. To help his own countrymen to understand the Scriptures, he wrote a book in which he showed how life in the Far North could give fresh and unexpected meanings to verses and passages that the reader had passed over almost without thinking. Such simple words as "rivers", "gold", "storms", and "pine trees" would suddenly glow with new life.

What should he call this last book, William wondered. Overhead the aurora was weaving and waving, dancing and shimmering across the sky, now sea green, now crimson, now blue. Suddenly William knew that he had found his title. He called the book *Northern Lights on the Bible*.

*   *   *

Great changes came to the lonely lands of the Far West beyond the Rockies. With the discovery of

gold along the Yukon River, miners came flocking
to the uninhabited country round its mouth. A
man working on the east side of the Rocky Mountains could not visit and supervise the mining
communities unless he was prepared to take a
journey of five thousand miles and to spend two
years away from the rest of his people.

There was only one thing to be done—the
Mackenzie River Diocese must be divided in its
turn. Again William wrote his urgent letters, and
again he was successful.

The eastern part kept the old name of Mackenzie
River. Now William had once more to make a
choice—would he go east or to the far north-west?
The Yukon called him, and once again he chose
the hard way.

In spite of the division, William Bompas had
still two hundred thousand square miles under his
care, an area rather more than twice the size of
Great Britain. His strange, wild, beautiful Yukon
was a land of bitter cold and burning heat, of
rugged mountains, impenetrable forests, dark blue
and dark green lakes, a paradise of flowers and
birds, a white and sinister winter world. For his
headquarters he chose a small township, sometimes called Buxton and sometimes Forty Mile
(after the river on which it stood). Situated at the
junction of the Yukon and the smaller river Forty
Mile, it was a good centre for his work.

Nina had returned from England by the time

her husband became Bishop of the Yukon. They
made their home in a mission house so dirty that
it needed much cleaning and a good deal of
patience before it could be lived in. William was a
busy man in those days. Instead of wall-paper he
pasted thick cotton twill over the walls and painted
the twill a brilliant red. "The colour gets sobered
down by degrees," poor Nina kept telling herself.
But she had to admit that the decoration of the
school-room was not an entire success. With the
thermometer standing at fifty degrees below zero,
the paste froze on the walls before it had time to
dry, and all the red-painted twill cracked. But they
soon were able to import a very good schoolmistress, who bore the cold so well that she
was only a little startled when her blanket at
night was fringed with icicles from her breath
freezing.

A good carpenter, William made shelves,
brackets, window-frames, dining-table, cupboard,
out of whatever wood he could find. When a coffin
was needed for an Indian brought from the
hunting-grounds for Christian burial, down came
the cupboard and the shelves, and the Bishop
made the coffin.

He waited on and helped everybody, and acted
as medical man. Nina did not approve of his
remedies. He *would* stick to his old calomel and
jalap, instead of exhibiting her up-to-date aconite,
belladonna and nux! If their patients improved,

she gave the praise to her remedies. If they got worse, she put the blame on his!

On the whole, Nina was very well satisfied with a house in which she could play the harmonium at family prayers if the keys did not happen to be frozen stiff. She liked living in a prettily-situated house on what was very nearly an island, with the mountains all round, range upon range. And when she wrote to her friends, she praised the "fine old Yukon".

Nina soon discovered that the fine old Yukon did not always behave as a noble river should. It could be, when it chose, the worst of neighbours. In spring, when the ice was melting, it rose fifty feet and that was the time when William must have wished to take back what he had said about the grand sight presented by the breaking up of ice in a great river.

More than once the household woke at night to hear the water swishing through the ground-floor rooms. Peeping out, they would see William's books and various other objects—caps, mittens, toys—swirling about in the flood.

On one night they were in grave danger. William brought all the children into a bedroom that over-looked the river. Warmly wrapped up, the little ones clung to one another, half fearful, half excited. To keep their spirits up, William made jokes and fed them with the tit-bits he had gone splashing downstairs to fetch when the water first trickled under the door. Then he told them Bible stories of brave people—Elisha and the horses and chariots of fire, the Three Children in the burning fiery furnace, Daniel in the den of lions. From time to time he broke off to lean through the open window to look and listen for any sign that rescue was at hand. At last, lights flashed on the dark heaving waters. Voices were heard—"Hi, there! We're coming!"

With utter disregard for their own safety, the Mounted Police had steered a boat through the floating ice. One by one William handed down five small furry bundles. They were followed by Nina. When his family were safely settled, William swung himself down into his place. Slowly, cautiously, the rescuers picked their way to the lanterns and torches that were guiding them landward. The boat bumped on wet grass in a field. Helpers rushed to drag it further in. Within minutes William, Nina and their children had found welcome and shelter among friends.

When the drying-out process was over, they all trooped home again. Theirs was a merry houseful, not unlike a miniature Tower of Babel, when three out of five Indian children spoke three different languages. The children found enjoyment in such simple occupations as filling the wood-boxes for the stove. In winter they liked carrying pails of water up to the house from the water-hole that William had to open every day with axe and chisel.

"Cold? It's not at all cold!" they assured Nina when they came prancing home from school in their wraps and fur mittens through a mid-day temperature of minus fifty.

Miners from the distant diggings spent the winter in Forty Mile when their "claims" were deep under snow and ice and they could no longer "pan" for gold either with their flat pans or their large box sluices. A rough-and-tough town it was, full of colourful characters with names like Salt-water Jack, Big Dick, Jimmy the Pirate, Buckskin Miller, Pete the Pig. "Cannibal" was so named because he liked to eat moose meat raw, chopping it off in hunks with his knife. "The Old Maiden" carried fifty pounds of newspapers with him wherever he went, " 'ca'se they's handy ter refer ter whin ye gits inter a' argymint". And there was Shoemaker Brown, who liked solitude. In the early days of mining when there were only sixty-five miners in the whole country, he sold his splendid "claim" ridiculously cheap. When he was asked why he did it—"Oh," said Brown, "they's gitten too thick for me round here!"

The miners had played so many disagreeable practical jokes on a young missionary stationed at Forty Mile that in the end his health and his mind both gave way, and he had to be taken back to England where he died. But nobody was likely to take any liberties with William, who was capable of breaking up a fight by pulling two men apart and dragging to a safe distance an aggressor who was armed with a long sharp knife. When he set up house at Forty Mile, his trouble was rather like Shoemaker Brown's. Forty Mile was rapidly becoming too "civilized" for a lover of the wilds.

Each succeeding year saw more miners crowding into Forty Mile. Stores where a man could buy everything from a bag of flour to a wedding-ring; six drinking saloons, a restaurant, billiard-room, distilleries for whisky and a horrible fiery spirit called *Hoochino*—Forty Mile had them all. In residence were two doctors, a blacksmith, a watchmaker and a dressmaker with the latest fashions.

Throughout the winter William did all he could to keep the Indians from drinking and gambling like the hard-living but often generous and kindly miners, not many of whom could be persuaded to come to his services, though they eagerly read the books that his friends in England sent out for them.

In summer he was glad to feel free to visit along the Yukon, it might be as far as Port Yukon or all the way to the Yukon's very mouth—if that wide area of swampy flats and intersecting channels could fairly be called a mouth. Here in Fort Yukon, almost on the edge of the world, a strange sight was seen by William during one of his trips. Bringing with him a large bowl of golden "eagles", a rich American came hoping to buy up the place.

His offers met with blank stares and puzzled head-shakings. "He offered his gold pieces (the almighty dollar)," William wrote home, "and they were declined as so much useless trash. They knew not what to do with them till one of the servants at last consented to receive a twenty-dollar piece to beat up into finger rings."

This happy ignorance pleased William, who longed to see men "greedy for the Gospel", and not for gold. But it did not last. Within a few years everyone in the Yukon knew very well what to do with gold.

Always in going and coming, William was bound to pass the spot where, fifty miles from the town of Forty Mile, the Klondike River joins the Yukon.

"Klondike" is thought to be a mispronunciation of the Indian word *Trondiuck* or "Hammer-water". The stream had a famous salmon run, and every year the Indians came to trap the fish by making barriers of stakes that were hammered or driven into the gravel bed of the river.

The meeting-point looked a place of peace, undisturbed, save by Indians camping there in summer for the fishing. Sometimes William's small band of missionaries would voyage between banks rich in golden vetch and magenta flowering-vine, and would land there to hold services for the fisher-folk. Much of the ground was a swamp hidden under a dense tangle of undergrowth, out of which stunted firs and spruces poked their heads. Driftwood lay thickly along the shores and in the creeks, one of which was named Rabbit

Creek. That place of peace was shortly to become a place of strife, holding out what the Canadian poet Robert Service called "a golden lure" to mankind.

7

GOLD, GOLD, GOLD!

ON August the sixteenth 1896 three men—George Carmack, Skookum Jim and Tagish Charley—were dancing madly round and round a gold-pan on Rabbit Creek. They flopped to the ground exhausted and stayed stretched out until they felt rested enough to begin adding to the four dollars' worth of gold in their pan. Men had reason to be hopeful if they made a quick find of only ten cents—but four dollars! That was a "strike", a sign maybe of riches untold. When they had filled an empty Winchester shotgun shell with pannings, they camped for the night. Carmack thought his thoughts. Skookum Jim and Tagish Charley chanted Indian songs of praise.

In the morning a pencilled notice appeared on a spruce tree:

TO WHOM IT MAY CONCERN

I do, this day, locate and claim, by right of discovery, five hundred feet, running upstream and from this notice. Located this seventeenth day of August 1896.

G. W. Carmack.

As soon as they had measured off and staked the claims for Skookum Jim and Tagish Charley and Carmack's second "discoverer's claim", the three men made for Forty Mile, where their claims had to be recorded at the police post. After five hours of struggling through thorny swamps, they reached the boat they had left hidden in a backwater. On their way downriver to the Yukon they encountered several discouraged miners, some of them almost starving. When the disappointed men heard the good news, they dashed helter-skelter to Rabbit Creek. These men, like the three discoverers, made their fortune.

On reaching Forty Mile, Carmack and his companions told the story again. Nobody believed them. Disbelief melted at sight of the gold. The miners melted away too. Salt-water Jack, Big Dick, Jimmy the Pirate, Buckskin Miller, Pete the Pig, Cannibal and the Old Maiden quietly disappeared. When morning dawned, the entire mining population of Forty Mile had taken itself off. Men too drunk to know what was happening were dragged aboard ship by their friends. Wild scenes of confusion, quarrelling, grabbing and cheating took place at Rabbit Creek. In the midst of their angry bawling, the miners spared time to call a meeting at which the creek was renamed Bonanza. They did not like Rabbit; it was a common sort of name!

The great Klondike Gold Rush had begun.

From distant diggings, from Circle City on the Alaskan border, from the other States, from England, from Africa, from Syria, from Australia, from Finland, Norway and Denmark, men came swarming in. The world was going mad with gold fever. Everywhere, the word of the day was "Klondike". Would-be gold-diggers who went nearly crazy in their struggles to get to the Klondike were said to be suffering from "klondicitis". Advertisements appeared on railway stations and on steamships: "Ho! For the Klondike!" Friends greeted one another with, "Klondike or bust!" Red-lettered lapel buttons were worn with "Yes, I'm going this spring" stamped on them.

In Victoria, Vancouver and elsewhere, shops took advantage of the boom to press their goods on the Klondikers. Chemists advertised their Klondike Medicines in bold headlines. "Every person going to Klondike should take a medicine chest. We have them already filled or will fill them to order." Ironmongers praised the superior quality of their "indurated fibreware" pails and pans, which were "endowed with a rugged constitution" and "added a handsome appearance to a sound body". Furriers urged the public to try their Klondike footwear. The wealthier gold-rushers bought special Stampeder outfits—thick cap, brightly-coloured mackinaw, thick boots—and took with them "Klondike" binoculars, stoves and blankets. Songs were sung about the streets:

All you miners wide awake!
Go to the Klondike, make your stake;
Get out your pick, your pan, your pack,
Go to the Klondike, don't come back.
Ho for the Klondike, Ho!

Within months the Indian fishing-village was transformed into a sea of white tents. Almost as swiftly it shot up into the city of Dawson with its houses, hospitals, theatre, fifteen drinking and gambling saloons, the Flora Dora and other dance halls. Evil men and women flocked to Dawson like so many birds of prey, panting to snatch what they could. Barmen panned the sawdust on the floors of the saloons for the gold dust that had fallen out of the miners' fat "pokes" of caribou skin. Children panned and sieved as busily as the barmen. Waiters purposely kept their hands damp so that gold flecks might stick to them when the customers paid their bills. The flecks were slipped into a pocket lined with chamois leather to be transferred later to a box.

Fortunes were made and gambled away by some of the gold-seekers. Others found nothing on their claims, and were left broken and destitute. The country could not feed the hordes that invaded it. At times famine prices were asked—a hundred dollars for a bag of flour. Men brought full pokes of gold dust, begging in vain for food for their wives and children. There were riots, near-riots, and disastrous, terrifying fires. When sickness broke out, the hospitals were filled with sufferers from typhoid, malaria and scurvy. Starving miners roamed the land in their wretchedness.

William had worked so long among Indians that he felt himself to be out of touch with white men, especially with those who had gold fever in their veins. Gold meant nothing at all to William, unless it was the scarlet and gold of the forest trees in autumn, or the golden tresses entwined with pearls of the Alexandra Falls, or the gold of Yukon wild flowers—yellow water crowfoot, arnica, cinquefoil, pond lily, Arctic poppy, yellow violet, mustard, golden corydales, loco weed and many others. He would gladly have given the miners the same message that the old Scottish minister Samuel Rutherford gave to the readers of his *Letters*:

> Acquaint yourself with Christ's love, and ye shall not miss to find new gold-mines and treasures in Christ.

William had found those gold-mines himself. He wrote to his brother George: "During the past winter, I have devoted my days to digging the mines of God's holy Word, and have found in my own estimation, richer prizes than the nuggets of Klondike."

The Indians treasured those Bible nuggets, though so many of the miners did not. They attended services on the coldest days, the children trotting alongside in their little rabbit-skin coats.

6

Some of the Indian men left Forty Mile and went to live in the forest the better to escape the temptation to drink the fiery stuff that drove them out of their senses. And once in their earnestness the young men came to William with an unusual problem. They made their living by the chase; hunting was all they knew. Was it wrong, then, to go hunting on Monday, so soon after partaking of Holy Communion?

But William did his valiant best to help the white men of Dawson and Forty Mile whose souls seemed thirsty for nothing but gold, gold, and more gold. Having accepted the fact that he now didn't understand non-Indians, he chose, from among his clergy and lay missionaries, just those men who could be of real use, and he placed them where they were most needed. Of the men sent to work in Dawson, one was a young clergyman, R. J. Bowen, whom William had himself trained and ordained. Mr. Bowen's friendly ways and handiness with a concertina won him an entrance to the miners' cabins and a corner in many of their hearts. With money sent out from England, William and Mr. Bowen built the first St. Paul's Church, a log church that was soon to be replaced by a bigger and better building.

Mr. Bowen had married Miss Mellett, the young schoolmistress who had been praised for standing the cold so well. When Nina visited them in their tiny house, she found a crowded church and "nice hearty services", proofs of William's wisdom in putting a round and not a square peg into a round hole. William was not happy at Dawson. He still thought so poorly of his own powers that he was often more depressed than he need have been. He tried to cheer himself with the assurance: "Christ reigns, and the work is His, not mine."

So he struggled on, in poor health and for a time in much anxiety about Nina, who had been summoned to England to nurse a sick sister. Returning by way of San Francisco, she found herself swallowed up in the Gold Rush.

Amid scenes of frenzied excitement, she boarded the first steamer conveying miners to the Klondike. The *Excelsior* took them as far as St. Michael, where they were transferred, after a tedious wait, to the small steamer *Alice*. At Fort Yukon the Captain announced that he wasn't going any further that year. He ordered all the passengers ashore, and there they had to remain till the river was open again in the following spring.

Once the ship had been cleared of the shouting, protesting passengers, the unscrupulous captain made off with his lightened ship! The missionary in charge at Fort Yukon acted swiftly. He put Nina into his own small boat and pursued the *Alice* up the river, calling on the Captain to stop. Nina called too. The Captain of the *Alice* heard but he would not heed their protests. She out-distanced them, and they were forced to turn wearily back.

The ninety passengers bestowed themselves as best they could in five or six small cabins belonging to the Fort. Nina had a curtained-off corner of the school-room that had been built by Fort Yukon's newly-arrived missionary, Mr. Hawkesly, who could not invite her to the mission house as it provided only two tiny bedrooms for his family of six. At night she felt very lonely and cold, with Arctic winds whistling round her, dogs howling, and wolves prowling about far too near to be agreeable. By day she had hard work to keep school for fifty children when the only equipment was a few broken slates and slate-pencils and some sheets of whitey-brown paper that she begged from the Hudson Bay Company's stores. To keep her turbulent pupils tolerably quiet, she had to invent for them endless thrilling stories about the adventures of two characters named Rose and Ben. When the frustrated Klondikers took to rioting against the American soldiers in charge of the Fort, she was terrified. Hunger and cold could be borne—but not this!

She had also a small private trouble of her own. Somehow or other William had contrived to get a letter to her in which he showed that he was vexed with her for failing to reach Forty Mile before winter. She might have made a more determined effort, William said.

Of course William did not know of her desperate chase up the river after the *Alice*! Nothing could have been more determined than that! But it was depressing to be blamed for what she could not help. After all, the long wait at St. Michael and the extraordinary behaviour of the *Alice*'s captain were no fault of hers.

That dreary winter came to an end at last. Nina returned to Forty Mile, bringing cheerfulness with her. She and William worked on, doing their best to help Indians and miners whenever and wherever they could . . . and then, as suddenly as it had begun, the Klondike Gold Rush was over. Word had come of a vast find of gold-dust on the sands of Nome, just across the Bering Strait from Siberia.

In a week eight thousand people stampeded out of Dawson, crowding on to the steamers that would take them down the Yukon to the new Eldorado. The houses were left empty, the dance halls and saloons were shut, the bright lights were gone. A few failed miners, unable or unwilling to make their way to Nome, lingered in the neighbourhood, some to find jobs, others to cling obstinately to the claims that would yield them barely enough to live on.

*   *   *

When the Gold Rush was fairly over, William had more time to give to his Indians. Up and down the Yukon he journeyed, and one whole winter he spent at the Indian village of Moosehide. He was growing old and tired when he went there, and the day of the long trips was nearly done, whether they were taken by canoe, steamer or his beloved dog-train. There would not be many more settings-forth in the dawn light after he had given his leading-dog the signal to start. "Forward!" "Off with you!" "Go ahead!" were all summed up in the one French word of command that was always used—*Marche!*

At Moosehide William made plans for the future. He resolved to leave the oversight of Forty Mile, Dawson, Whitehorse and the rest to the care of the active young men he had chosen, all helpers whom he could trust. For himself, he would go south. At Caribou Crossing—soon to be known as Carcross—there were Indians to whom an ageing bishop could minister. Carcross, on the shores of Lake Bennett had both steamers and railway station; he would be able to send and receive letters frequently instead of only twice a year at the most. Yes, Carcross was the place for him!

It was a change from the years when he had deliberately chosen to plunge deeper and deeper into Arctic solitude. But it was a strictly limited change. There was life in him yet, and he refused to go to England even for a visit, let alone for retirement. He told a friend, "On the whole a visit to England would be painful to me after so many changes, and I do not expect again to cross the water. I feel to be a naturalized North American."

One final piece of work remained to be done. Before he left Forty Mile in the summer of 1901, he heard that smallpox had broken out in what remained of Dawson City. His friends at Moosehide were in danger, and he hurried there at once.

The Indians were suspicious when they saw him coming with what looked like a doctor's little black bag.

"What's that for? He means business of some kind, I can see that," one Indian remarked to the others with him.

"I reckon I know. It's that smallpox in Dawson," came the reply. "He's going to vaccinate us to prevent us catching it. I met a man from Fort Simpson once, an old man he was, who told me what the Bishop did up there before he was a bishop if you know what I mean. I'll tell you—"

"No, you needn't. I've heard of vaccination before and I don't like the thought of it. I won't have it done to me."

"I won't, either."

"Nor will I."

The Indians of Fort Simpson could have told the Indians of Moosehide that they were simply wasting their breath. Calmly but firmly William Bompas insisted on vaccinating them all!

8

AT HOME IN THE LOGHOUSE

WILLIAM and Nina had arrived in Carcross with their small stock of goods and the big tent they had prudently borrowed from their friend Bishop Ridley. Carcross was only a small place, and when the up-river steamer brought them to the landing-stage they did not know whether they would be able to find an empty house.

They were alone; for William had reluctantly decided that he and his wife were no longer young and strong enough to take charge of children. After all, they had reached the age when most married couples are grand-parents! And grand-parents couldn't be expected to cope with the kind of emergencies that were all too likely to happen when children were about. As, for instance, Baby Mary's prank when, feeling in need of a drink, she toddled down to the edge of the mighty River Yukon to get it—and was caught just in time! And there was the equally bad day when Frisky, aged eight, took a day off from school without warning. She climbed out of her bedroom window and stole into the woods, the excuse she made being her desire to pick berries and to think "long thoughts" about a brother who had died. When she was tired of rambling about, she took possession of a miner's empty cabin and stole from his store of food. At night she sauntered home, singing; but when she drew near the house, she not unnaturally felt shy about entering. So she climbed into an old crooked tree and went peacefully to sleep, not forgetting to say the verse that all the children repeated before they slept. Meanwhile the search-party and the Mounties had searched to no purpose . . .

No, decidedly the time had come to give up child-care!

But they couldn't quite make up their minds to do without children altogether. It had already been arranged that Miss Ellis, schoolmistress at Forty Mile, should bring down her resident children as soon as a suitable house could be found for them.

William and Nina made inquiries. They heard that on the other side of the lake there was a house large enough to take the school. On this side there was a derelict empty house that had been an inn and afterwards a post-office. They bought it for thirty pounds.

This truly remarkable bargain had two large rooms, a kitchen, and two small offices, one of which had the postmaster's desk still in it. The floorboards were half an inch apart, and the light of heaven shone through the roof. As dirty as their former residence at Forty Mile, it was full of mice

and squirrel-like gophers, thieves every one of
them. The mice at least had the politeness to do
their thieving unobtrusively, but the gophers had
no shame. After each theft they sprang on to the
rafters and sat there, grinning saucily. Empty
bottles were piled up thickly round the house.

It was a really horrid sight. Nina turned away to
look at the mountains beyond the lake. She found
that the mountains always had power to calm and
soothe her; for the beauty of their outlines, their
ever-varying tints and shadows, the mystery of
their dark fissures, the rapture of their glory at
sunsets all spoke to her of God, "Who in His
strength setteth fast the mountains and is girded
about with power".

After looking at the mountains, William and
Nina had to think about getting rid of the bottles.
An Indian lad showed signs of interest.

"Will you throw them into the lake for us? At
fifty cents an hour?"

"Sure."

He borrowed a wheelbarrow and began piling
up the bottles. Smash, crash, splash! After three
hours the work was done. The cleaning operations,
however, took longer.

A "bush telegraph" told the Indians at a distance that the Bishop had come. So they came too,
pitching their tents along the lakeside. Out came
the Bishop's medicine chest. He treated all manner
of complaints, including the mysterious ailment of

a patient who demanded "strong medicine in case he should be ill next winter".

"What's wrong with you?" asked William.

"Nothing. I'm quite well."

"What's likely to go wrong next winter? Rheumatism, bronchitis, or what?"

"How should I know what will be wrong with me next winter when I'm not ill now? Give me strong medicine to cure it, whatever it may be."

*　　　*　　　*

It was all very well for William to protest that there were to be no more children in his house. They were in and out of the Mission house all day. "Dear little dark-eyed gypsies, full of fun and mischief," Nina called them. Elder girls came to her for training in housewifery and needlecraft. And soon William was hard at work making wooden bedsteads, benches, chairs and tables for Miss Ellis and her troop.

But in making his arrangements for a school on the other side of the lake, William had overlooked the all-important fact that the bridge belonging to the Yukon and White Pass Railway lay between the school and the Carcross store. The sleepers were set so far apart that the blue waters of storm-ridden Lake Bennett could be seen dancing and churning beneath them—but no power on earth could keep those children from skipping lightly across to buy their five cents' worth of candy at the store. They did not even skip faster when a train thundered round the bend.

The Mounted Police had their barracks close to the mission house. William could not rest till he had persuaded the kind-hearted Mounties to change quarters with his terrible children!

He taught daily in the little school that was to grow after his death into the famous residential school for Indian children, Chooutla. When money was needed to build a church in Carcross, his appeals brought money from England and else-where, and he himself was in the team of builders. In other ways he worked as hard as he had ever done, though his teaching and preaching were, as a rule, carried on near home. In his intense dislike of putting himself forward, he shrank even from having his photograph taken. "I don't want to see *you* go," he said to one of his clergy, "but I should like to see your *camera* make a hasty departure."

Once, however, he was obliged to go down to Winnipeg to attend a conference of bishops. While he was in the city he was coaxed into addressing a large missionary meeting. The chairman began by praising the wonderful deeds of "our hero of the North". It was very difficult to make a hero out of William. When the chairman talked about the hardships of a pioneer missionary's life, William interrupted at once. "No, no," said William. "It is you men at the centre with your telephones and your telegrams, who have the hardships. We have a soft time in the North. Nobody ever worries us."

Then he went home to his log-house and his books. He and Nina had not much in the way of furniture, and his best chair was made out of an old barrel by the Carcross schoolboys, with cushioning and upholstering by Miss Ellis. But whatever else was missing, the Bompases always contrived to have plenty of books. Nina, who was an Italian scholar, carried Dante's *The Divine Comedy* in her pocket to the end of her life.

*   *   *

William's iron strength ebbed away till he found he could no longer watch over his great diocese as in the past. He resigned his office, but he was anxious to be active after he had left Carcross. When he thought of opening a new mission station among the Indians on Little Salmon River, it had to be gently explained to him that he was not strong enough for such an undertaking.

"Very well," said William. "I'll go back to Forty Mile. I can still do a little work there."

So it was arranged. All was made ready for the coming of the new Bishop, I. O. Stringer; reports, letters, papers and accounts were in perfect order —nothing was left undone. William and Nina had packed their boxes and had booked passages on the steamer for themselves and two Indian girls who were with them.

Saturday came, a calm, sunny June Saturday. They were due to leave on the Monday. That Saturday William was as energetic as ever; it was noticed that he strode along with the step of a young man. He went twice to the school and once to the Indian encampment to visit some sick people. He had long talks with Bishop Stringer, who had arrived and was staying in the house. At night, after he had read prayers, William went to his study to finish preparing the farewell sermon he was to preach on the Sunday.

Some little help was needed in the house. William Bompas rose to give it. As he did so, he swayed and staggered. Arms were round him before he could fall, and he was tenderly lowered to the floor. For a few moments he lay there unconscious, not moving. Then Bishop Stringer saw that he was no longer with them. Only the worn-out body remained, soon to be laid to rest in the forest graveyard among his Indian friends. But the old leader had heard a command meant for him alone—*Marche!*

Acknowledgment is made to Messrs. Seeley, Service & Co. for permission to quote from H. A. Cody's "Apostle of the North" and to the S.P.C.K. for permission to quote from "A Heroine of the North".